The Way Back
— to —
God's Kingdom

A Story of Sacrifice, — Refreshment, and New Life —

Rev. DeLante Dates

ISBN: 979-8-218-90637-5 (paperback)
       979-8-218-93263-3 (ebook)

First printing, 2026

Contents

Preface vii

Chapter 1. **FAR FROM THE KINGDOM** 1

Chapter 2. **THE CHILD AT THE POOL** 5

Chapter 3. **A ROAD NO ONE WANTED** 9

Chapter 4. **THIRTY-THREE YEARS IN THE SAND** 13

Chapter 5. **IT IS FINISHED** 17

Chapter 6. **THE NARROW GATE** 21

Chapter 7. **THE GATE GUIDE** 25

Chapter 8. **HEAT OF THE JOURNEY** 29

Chapter 9. **THE REFRESHMENT BOOTHS** 33

Chapter 10. **COVERED IN THE DESERT** 37

Chapter 11. **THE POOL BEYOND WORDS** 41

Chapter 12. **THE KING WHO BUILT THE WAY** 45

Chapter 13. **Closing Prayer** 49

Chapter 14. **Benediction** 50

PREFACE

This book was born from a vivid dream I had in 2018, one that stayed with me long after I awoke. In it, I saw a desert, a road, a narrow gate, and living water. I witnessed sacrifice, struggle, perseverance, and restoration—and I realized I was seeing more than a dream. I was seeing the Gospel come to life.

The desert reflected humanity's separation from God. The road revealed the way made through sacrifice. The gate symbolized faith, and the water represented the grace that sustains us on the journey home. Through it all, I saw the story of Jesus Christ, who left glory, entered our wilderness, endured the cross, and made a way back to the Father.

That message connected deeply with my own life. Raised in a small Pentecostal church in Southeast Washington, D.C., I was shaped by faith, prayer, and service, even while witnessing the brokenness and spiritual hunger surrounding my community during the crack epidemic of the late 1980s and early 1990s. Those experiences planted a question in my heart: **"What is the purpose of my life?"**

As I journeyed through college, marriage, and ministry, my search for purpose became a deeper pursuit of God. Alongside my wife, I grew in faith and service, discovering that true purpose is found in walking with Christ and helping others find hope in Him.

This book is not meant to replace Scripture, but to illuminate its truth through story. My prayer is that, like me, you will recognize yourself somewhere along this journey. And if you ever find your heart longing for the water, questioning the road, or pausing before the gate, remember this: the way has already been prepared, and the King who built it is waiting for you.

CHAPTER 1

FAR FROM THE KINGDOM

Key Scripture: Isaiah 59:2

The desert spread far beyond the eye's vision. Sand rolled in all directions, moving upward and downward like frozen ripples in time. The sun hung high in the sky, crushing down on everything below it. Life existed here, but it was difficult, characterized not by richness but by perseverance. People learned early on how to exist with little and how to ration hope in the same manner that they rationed water.

Few people speak of the Kingdom anymore, not because it didn't exist, but because it seemed too far away to matter. Stories about its beauty were passed down for many generations: lush agriculture, tranquility that did not fade with the night, and an enormous pool whose waters never ran dry. Some claimed that the water rejuvenated strength. Others claimed it could heal wounds that the desert could not. However, for most, the Kingdom had become little more than a story told to children when the heat became intolerable.

"But your iniquities have separated you from your God;
your sins have hidden His face from you."
— **Isaiah 59:2 NIV**

Even tales leave traces. Whispers moved through the dusty landscape like the wind, quietly yet relentlessly. Travelers described a land beyond the beach where water reflected the sky and delight did not fade with the morning dew. These whispers triggered something deep within the humans, an agony they couldn't describe. Though many disregarded the stories as naive optimism, others found themselves looking to the horizon and wondering whether life was intended to be greater than mere survival.

"He has also set eternity in the human heart."
— **Ecclesiastes 3:11 NIV**

Among those who lived closest to the desert's edge stood a large lake, an oasis that matched anything else. Its waters were pure, limitless, and vibrant. The sun touched it but never exhausted it. Time passed, yet the pool remained unchanged.

A child played on the border of this pool within the Kingdom. He walked effortlessly through the water, laughing, diving beneath the surface, and resurfacing rejuvenated each time. The water seemed to know him and embrace him. Where others would have given up, his determination made him stronger. To him, the pool was not a mystery; it was his home.

"For with You is the fountain of life;
in Your light we see light."
— **Psalm 36:9 NIV**

One day, as the child relaxed by the pool's edge, he looked out from the protection of the Kingdom and across the vast barren land beyond its borders. Despite the abundance around him, a calm sadness settled in his heart.

"Father," he declared softly but sincerely, "I wish I had brothers and sisters to share this pool with." The Father, standing next to him, followed the child's gaze to the wide expanse of sand beyond the water's edge. He had seen the desert long before the child mentioned it. He understood the distance and recognized the danger. With compassion in his eyes, the Father replied softly, "They are out there. The journey is far, and the journey is harsh." The child's brow furrowed. "Can they not come?"

The Father turned toward a weathered sign standing at the edge of the Kingdom, marking the divide between abundance and barrenness. Its words were carved deep, worn by time and wind:

THE KINGDOM LIES BEYOND.

Beneath it, faint yet unmistakable, were etched the words everyone dreaded:

NO ROAD EXISTS.

"How, then, can they call on the One they have not believed in? And how can they believe in the One of whom they have not heard?"
— **Romans 10:14 NIV**

The Father continued, "A road must be made to reach them." It would not be an easy route either. The child remained silent. His gaze never left the desert as he sat at the edge of the pool, still within the Kingdom and surrounded by life. A decision that would alter everything began to take shape in that silence, not out of lack, but out of love.

*"Then I said, 'Here I am—it is written about Me in the scroll—
I have come to do Your will, My God.'"*
— **Hebrews 10:7 NIV**

Unaware that a route back to the Kingdom was about to be created, the people of the desert continued with their lives, separate from one another. And their journey home was well underway, even though they could not see it yet.

Reflection Questions — Chapter 1: Far From the Kingdom

1. In what ways does the desert in this chapter reflect spiritual separation or distance from God?
2. Why do you think people stopped speaking about the Kingdom?
3. What does the pool represent in your own life?
4. How does the child's longing for others challenge individualistic faith?
5. What "no road exists" signs have you believed in your own journey with God?

Prayer Prompts — Chapter 1: Far From the Kingdom

- Lord, reveal where distance has formed between my heart and Your Kingdom.
- Help me recognize the longing You placed within me for more than survival.
- Awaken my hope for the life You intended me to live.

CHAPTER 2

THE CHILD AT THE POOL

Key Scripture: John 4:14

Morning light danced across the surface of the pool, scattering reflections like living jewels. While the desert awoke slowly, groaning under the promise of another scorching day, the water remained calm, steady, and full. Nothing in the desert could steal from it. Nothing could exhaust it.

The child entered the water once more. Each step into the pool restored what the desert had no power to give. Strength returned. Peace settled. Where the sand wore people down grain by grain, the water rebuilt him entirely. This pool was not merely a place of relief; it was a source.

"Whoever drinks the water that I shall give him will never thirst."
— John 4:14 NKJV

From the pool's edge, the child could easily see the desert. He watched the people move beneath the sun, burdened and fatigued, not realizing that such refreshment was so close yet so far away. They labored endlessly, searching for shade and wells that dried up as quickly as they were discovered.

Heaviness filled his heart. Though the pool gave him life, joy was incomplete without others sharing it. The laughter that echoed across the water seemed incomplete, as though it were meant to be duplicated.

"It is not good that the man should be alone."
— **Genesis 2:18 KJV**

The child raised his eyes toward the Kingdom beyond the desert, where the Father dwelled in fullness. He knew the Father's heart. He knew the Kingdom was never meant for one person.

Father, he said quietly, they are weary. The Father did not answer immediately. His silence was not lack of indifference, but sorrow. Together, they watched as a man in the distance collapsed beneath the weight of the heat, his strength spent, his hope nearly gone.

"Come to Me, all you who labor and are heavy laden, and I will give you rest."
— **Matthew 11:28 NKJV**

The Father placed His hand upon the child's shoulder. "I know," he said. "I have always known."

The child turned fully toward the desert, his eyes steady, his resolve growing. "Then send Me."

The words hung in the air, heavier than the heat, weightier than the sand. The Father looked at the child with love that stretched deeper than the pool itself. He saw not just the desert, but also the road that would eventually cross it. He understood the cost before it was paid.

"For God so loved the world that He gave His one and only Son."
— **John 3:16 NIV**

"If you go," the Father said, "You will not return unchanged." The child nodded. He wasn't expecting to.

The pool shimmered behind him, but the child continued to gaze forward. The road starts somewhere between the water and the Kingdom. And though no one else could yet see it, the child had already stepped towards the desert.

Reflection Questions — Chapter 2: The Child at the Pool

1. Why is the pool described as a source rather than merely a place of relief?
2. What does the child's willingness to leave the pool reveal about love and sacrifice?
3. How does this chapter reflect Christ's compassion for weary humanity?
4. What comforts or "pools" might God be asking you to step away from for the sake of others?
5. How does understanding the cost of the road deepen your gratitude for salvation?

Prayer Prompts — Chapter 2: The Child at the Pool

- Jesus, thank You for leaving glory to bring me living water.
- Show me where comfort has caused me to forget compassion for others.
- Align my heart with Your willingness to sacrifice for love.

CHAPTER 3

A ROAD NO ONE WANTED

Key Scripture: Isaiah 53:3

The desert refused to accept the plans. It resisted change in the same way it resisted rain, exerting effort before surrendering to silence. When word circulated that a road would be built through the sand, a mental shift occurred, creating doubt in some. Other people chuckled at the idea. Some shook their heads in sympathy, while others became furious, as if the concept itself were a violation of the desert's norms. They scoffed, even though they were there.

They had learned to accept the sand. It was familiar, unpleasant, but anticipated. A road signified disruption. A road meant hope, but hope had disappointed them before.

"Can anything good come from there?"
— **John 1:46 NIV**

Still, the work began.

The journey began as the child stepped completely into the desert and committed to the Father's purpose. He did not have the arsenal of tools that people expected. He carried no map, no army, and no declaration of authority. He carried obedience, and the desert had never been able to stop it.

Every day, the sun bore down on Him like it does on everyone else. Every move forward demanded more than just authority; it required commitment. Sand shifted beneath His feet, undoing all that had been done the day before. Progress was slow and uncomfortable, and at times it was obscure, but he remained determined to fulfill his mission.

"He is despised and rejected by men,
a Man of sorrows and acquainted with grief."
— **Isaiah 53:3 NKJV**

Those who passed by mocked Him. Some called Him foolish. Others warned Him to stop before He ruined His life. A few tried to block the work altogether, fearing what might happen if the road were finished. They did not know where it led; they only knew it challenged the way things had always been.

"The stone the builders rejected
has become the cornerstone."
— **Psalm 118:22 NIV**

Why would anyone choose to follow this road, they questioned. The child never argued; he simply continued building the road. With every stretch of ground cleared, the road grew, not wide, not smooth, but firm. It pointed steadily towards the Kingdom, though few were willing to follow it. From a distance, it looked unnecessary. Up close, it looked costly. At times, even the desert itself seemed to rise against him. Heat pressed harder, nights grew colder, and the work demanded everything: his time, his strength, and his comfort. Still, he pressed on, driven by the image of brothers and sisters laughing together at the pool.

"For the joy set before Him, He endured the cross."
— **Hebrews 12:2 NIV**

Years passed. The road became longer, stretching farther into the desert than anyone had ever dreamed possible. Many who had once mocked became silent. Others walked away completely, refusing to see something they couldn't understand. And though the road was still unfinished, one reality had emerged:

This was not a road the people asked for; It was the road they needed.

Reflection Questions — Chapter 3: A Road No One Wanted

1. Why do people often resist the ways God provides for salvation?
2. How have you experienced misunderstanding or opposition while obeying God?
3. What fears arise when hope disrupts familiar patterns?
4. Why is faithfulness more important than public approval?
5. How does this chapter challenge the idea that God's way should always feel comfortable?

Prayer Prompts — Chapter 3: A Road No One Wanted

- Father, give me courage to trust Your way even when it is misunderstood.
- Help me endure when obedience feels costly and unseen.
- Teach me to value faithfulness over approval.

CHAPTER 4

THIRTY-THREE YEARS IN THE SAND

Key Scripture: Luke 2:52

The road wasn't expanding quickly. One challenging step at a time, it stretched ahead with every mile achieved by labor that few saw and even fewer appreciated. Days turned into years, and years became something more meaningful than just mere existence. The desert turned into an acquaintance, persistent, relentless, and constantly demanding more than it provided.

The child grew as the road grew. His hands, once smooth, became marked by labor. His body encountered the weight of weariness. Yet his eyes never lost their focus. He remained fixed on the Kingdom, even when the sand blurred the horizon, he kept his eyes set on the Kingdom.

"And Jesus grew in wisdom and stature,
and in favor with God and man."
— Luke 2:52 NIV

In what seemed like a single, continuous journey, thirty-three years flew by. Each year had its own weight. On particular days, peaceful times of spending time with the Father made the job feel lighter. On other days, the desert put a greater strain on His body and determination.

"In the days of His flesh, Jesus offered up prayers and supplications, with loud cries and tears."
— **Hebrews 5:7 ESV**

The desert inhabitants were more conscious of the passing of time than the development of the road. They observed His aging. They witnessed the cost of the labor. Some felt sorry for him. He was written off by others as a man who had wasted his life pursuing something that no one had requested. A couple were curious but unwilling to commit, so they followed from a distance.

"He came to His own, and His own did not receive Him."
— **John 1:11 NKJV**

Nevertheless, he continued to be devoted. Now, the road stretched farther than any previous road. It formed a limited but distinct route through the middle of the desert. Although unfinished, it carried a promise:

There is a way.

The child, now fully a man, stood one evening at the edge of the work, looking back at the path behind him and forward toward what remained. He knew that the hardest part was yet to come. The road demanded more than time. It demanded everything..

*"No one takes [My life] from Me,
but I lay it down of My own accord."*
— **John 10:18 NIV**

He was surrounded by stillness as the desert cooled and the sun dropped. In that silence, He addressed the Father with words of surrender rather than complaint. He whispered, "It's not my will, but it's yours."

"Yet not as I will,
but as You will."
— **Matthew 26:39 NIV**

The route remained unfinished, but the goal was evident. Thirty-three years spent in the sand had not gone to waste. They had set the ground for sacrifice, completion, and an unforgettable moment in the desert. The Kingdom waited. And so did the cost.

Reflection Questions — Chapter 4: Thirty-Three Years in the Sand

1. What does long-term obedience look like in your own life?
2. How do seasons of waiting shape your faith?
3. Why is surrender often harder than action?
4. In what ways does unseen faithfulness prepare us for future purposes?
5. How does Jesus' endurance change how you view your own struggles?

Prayer Prompts — Chapter 4: Thirty-Three Years in the Sand

- Lord, teach me the value of faithfulness over time.
- Help me trust You in seasons when progress feels slow or unseen.
- Give me strength to surrender my will to Yours, even when obedience is costly.

CHAPTER 5

IT IS FINISHED

Key Scripture: John 19:30

The sky changed without anyone noticing. What began as an ordinary day in the desert gradually became heavy, as if creation itself knew what was about to happen. The sun continued to shine, but its radiance was muted by a sorrow beyond words.

The road now stretched from the pool's edge well into the desert. It was complete. Not wide. Not easy. But unbroken.

At the end of the road, there was a thin, upright gate that was easily identifiable. It did not blend into the scenery or compete for attention. It simply stood there waiting. Anyone who reached it would understand what it was.

The man who built the road stood under the weight of the moment. His physique carried the signs of the voyage, with years of obedience engraved into flesh and bone. Every step, every particle of sand moved, has led to this point. The desert remained silent, as if it had also been humbled.

"And being found in appearance as a man,
He humbled Himself by becoming obedient to death."
— Philippians 2:8 NIV

The crowd gathered, some out of curiosity, some out of mistrust. Few understood what they were seeing. They saw fatigue, not success. They saw weakness rather than fulfillment. But Father saw things differently.

The man lifted. His gaze was drawn to the sky, to the Kingdom that had never left Him, even when surrounded by the desert. He yelled out, "It is finished," louder than the desert winds, uncertainty, or fear.

"When He had received the drink, Jesus said, 'It is finished.'
With that, He bowed His head and gave up His spirit."
— John 19:30 NIV

And then he collapsed. The ground beneath him trembled, not with power, but with finality. The road no longer held hope. It was reality. The road no longer held hope. The gate was no longer waiting to be erected; it was open to anyone who would come. What no one realized at the time was that the collapse did not equal defeat. It was completion.

"By one sacrifice He has made perfect forever
those who are being made holy."
— Hebrews 10:14 NIV

The desert, once a place of separation, now held a way back to the Kingdom. The road had been paid for in full. And though the Builder lay still, His work spoke louder than any voice ever could.

Reflection Questions — Chapter 5: It Is Finished

1. What does *"It is finished"* mean for your salvation today?
2. Why is it difficult to rest in complete grace instead of striving?
3. How does understanding Christ's sacrifice change your identity?
4. What burdens are you still carrying that Jesus has already paid for?
5. How does the finished road redefine your journey toward God's Kingdom?

Prayer Prompts — Chapter 5: It Is Finished

- Jesus, thank You for finishing the work I could never complete.
- Help me trust that nothing needs to be added to Your sacrifice.
- Teach me to rest in what You have already done.

CHAPTER 6

THE NARROW GATE

Key Scripture: Matthew 7:13–14

After the road was completed, many expected the journey to be over. They believed that the end of the sacrifices meant the end of walking. But instead of a wide opening, the road led them to something unexpected: a gate. It stood at the end of the long, hard-built path, quiet yet unmistakable. It was narrow, not because it was hidden, but because it was intentionally designed that way. No one could rush through it. No one could carry excess with them. The gate required attention.

"Enter through the narrow gate. For wide is the gate and broad is the road that leads to destruction."
— **Matthew 7:13–14 NIV**

At the gate stood a guide. He did not block the entrance or hurry people through. He stood watch, not as a guard to keep people out, but as someone tasked with clearing the way. His voice was calm, steady, and confident.

"The only requirement to enter," he told me, "is to admit that you believe this path is the way." Nothing was asked concerning the amount of time they had walked. Nothing was required regarding what they endured through. Belief was the entry.

"Jesus answered, 'I am the way and the truth and the life. No one comes to the Father except through Me.'"
— **John 14:6 NIV**

"If you confess with your mouth, 'Jesus is Lord,' and believe in your heart that God raised Him from the dead, you will be saved."
— **Romans 10:9 CSB**

Some hesitated. They had traveled a long way and were expecting the gate to swing open automatically. Others grappled with the requirement's simplicity. They sought proof, explanation, or reassurance beyond belief. However, the gate did not negotiate. It did not adjust to the individual's requests. It stood steady, unaffected by opinion or pressure. Those who believed came forward. When they passed through, the guide spoke again, not as a warning, but as preparation.

"This journey may still feel long," he explained. "The heat will bear down on you. You will become fatigued. There will be moments in which you feel discouraged, lonely, or tempted to turn back." His words were not meant to intimidate them, but rather to anchor them. "Along the way," he declared, "there are refreshment booths placed to give you strength and hope. Use them. Do not ignore them. They have been provided to help you endure."

"Come to Me, all who are weary and burdened, and I will give you rest."
— **Matthew 11:28 NASB**

"And surely I am with you always, to the very end of the age."
— **Matthew 28:20 NIV**

Those who persevered quickly realized that something had changed. Although they were still in the desert, the heat no longer crushed them the way it once had. After receiving refreshment, a covering seemed to rest over them, a shield they had not carried before. The sun still burned, but it no longer defeated them. They were protected.

"The Lord is your keeper... the sun shall not strike you by day."
— **Psalm 121:5–6 NKJV**

They understood that the gate was not the end of the journey. It was only the beginning of the walk. The narrow gate had not restricted them. It had secured them.

"I am the gate; whoever enters through Me will be saved."
— **John 10:9 NIV**

Reflection Questions — Chapter 6: The Narrow Gate

1. Why do you think the gate is described as narrow but obvious?
2. What makes trusting the gate difficult for some people?
3. What baggage are you carrying through that gate that is making your journey harder than God intended?
4. How does faith, rather than effort, redefine entrance into God's Kingdom?
5. What does walking through the gate symbolize in your own spiritual journey?

Prayer Prompt — Chapter 6: The Narrow Gate

- Lord, help me trust the narrow way even when it feels uncomfortable.
- Teach me to release what I cannot carry into Your Kingdom.
- Thank You for the protection and refreshment You provide along the way.

CHAPTER 7

THE GATE GUIDE

Key Scripture: John 16:13

Those who passed through the narrow gate expected answers. They had reached the end of the road they could see, yet before them stretched another path—longer, quieter, marked by trust rather than signage. The desert still surrounded them, but something within them had shifted. The desert heat no longer felt like punishment. It felt like proof they were still moving.

The guide waited just outside the gate. He was not intimidating in appearance, and he was not trying to gain respect through force. His presence was constant and calming, like a shade that emerged just when it was needed. Those who stared at him felt heard, as if he understood their journey before they even said a word.

"When He, the Spirit of truth, comes, He will guide you into all truth."
— John 16:13 NIV

Some people immediately started asking him questions. "How long will the trip be? Will the desert ever end? What if I become tired and turn back?" The guide listened patiently. He did not discount their anxieties. Instead, he acknowledged them with compassion.

"The journey may feel long," he said. "There will be days when the sun presses harder than others. You will feel weak. You may feel alone. But you are not abandoned."

"For all who are led by the Spirit of God are children of God."
— **Romans 8:14 NLT**

He pointed to the route ahead. "You will learn to walk differently today, relying on trust rather than sight. When the desert beckons you to stop, remember the path beneath your feet. It was finished before you ever stepped on it.

The people traveling observed something else. The guide did not walk ahead or behind them. He strolled alongside them, altering his pace to match the slowest of them, never rushing and never leaving anyone behind unless they wanted to stop.

"The Lord is close to the brokenhearted and saves those who are crushed in spirit."
— **Psalm 34:18 NIV**

The guide would occasionally point to little shelters along the road that provided refreshment, relaxation, and rejuvenation when the heat got too bad. They appeared unimportant from a distance. They become lifelines up close.

He said, "You'll need these." Endurance is not the only source of strength.

"My grace is sufficient for you, for My power is made perfect in weakness."
— **2 Corinthians 12:9 NIV**

A few travelers hesitated, embarrassed to acknowledge that they were exhausted so soon after entering the gate. The guide greeted them with kindness. He told them, "Rest is not failure. It's wisdom." They remained subjected to the struggle in the desert, but the journey no longer seemed pointless. Every step had significance. Every instance of weakness served as a call to greater trust.

Many of them came to the poignant realization that the guide was doing more than just pointing them in the right direction. He was preparing them for their return to the kingdom.

"[Those who are led by the Spirit] are being transformed into His image."
— 2 Corinthians 3:18 NIV

Reflection Questions — Chapter 7: The Gate Guide

1. How does the guide's presence change the experience of the journey?
2. In what ways have you sensed guidance during difficult seasons?
3. Why is it important that the guide walks with the travelers rather than ahead of them?
4. How does rest play a role in spiritual growth?
5. What does being led require from you personally?

Prayer Prompt — Chapter 7: The Gate Guide

- Holy Spirit, guide me when the path feels uncertain.
- Help me recognize Your presence in every step of my journey.
- Teach me to rest without guilt and walk without fear.

CHAPTER 8

HEAT OF THE JOURNEY

Key Scripture: John 16:33

The gate did not make travel any easier. The route stretched farther than many had anticipated as it proceeded through the desert. The sand continued to shift under their feet, and the sun continued to rise every day. Some believed that going through the gate would put an end to the conflict, but they quickly discovered that the gate provided direction rather than eliminating the journey.

Before the road, movement had meant little. Even after years of walking, they never really got anywhere. Every step was important now, though. They were no longer wandering aimlessly, because the desert still existed. Beneath them, the road remained unwavering, pointing ahead when the horizon offered no clues.

"In this world you will have trouble. But take heart! I have overcome the world."
— **John 16:33 NIV**

The heat initially brought up memories of the past. Slowly, fatigue set in. Once more, doubt whispered. Discouragement attempted to remind them of how far they still needed to go. They did not, however, predict which way to turn or walk in circles as they had in the past. The road itself attested to the fact that they were heading in the direction of the truth.

Then they noticed a refreshment booth. It was straightforward, deliberate, and impossible to mistake for an accident as it stood beside the road. Water, shade, and rest were waiting for all who came. There was no need to pay; there was no precondition. It had all been provided.

"He restores my soul; He leads me in paths of righteousness for His name's sake."
— **Psalm 23:3 NKJV**

People who drank experienced a return to their strength in both their bodies and their hearts. Where fatigue had taken hold, hope reappeared. What had previously seemed unreasonable now seemed achievable. A few attempted to walk by the booth without pausing. They convinced themselves that they could go without rest because they were strong enough, disciplined enough, or far enough along. However, those who refused provision were humbled by the desert. Many eventually came back, exhausted, thirsty, and eager to accept what had been generously given.

"We are hard pressed on every side, but not crushed; perplexed, but not in despair."
— **2 Corinthians 4:8 NIV**

"My grace is sufficient for you, for My power is made perfect in weakness."
— **2 Corinthians 12:9 NIV**

As they continued, they noticed something else. After each time they stopped to receive refreshment, the sun seemed less harsh.

The heat no longer pressed down on them in the same way. Though the desert had not changed, they had. A covering rested over them, a shield they did not carry themselves. Obedience was followed by protection. The road beneath their feet remained firm, unmoved by wind or doubt, guiding them forward when uncertainty threatened to blur their vision.

"The Lord will guard you from all evil; He will keep your soul."
— **Psalm 121:7**

They learned an important truth on that stretch of the road: The journey was not sustained by endurance alone, nor by direction alone, but by frequently returning to the places of refreshment along the way. There were no detours at the booths. They were incorporated into the design. And those who learned to pause, drink, and relax discovered that the road did more than carry them forward; it prevented them from getting lost again.

*"He who began a good work in you will carry it on
to completion."*
— **Philippians 1:6 NIV**

Reflection Questions — Chapter 8: Heat of the Journey

1. Why doesn't the desert disappear after entering the path?
2. How have challenges tested your faith since choosing to follow Christ?
3. What does this chapter teach about endurance versus self-reliance?
4. How can discouragement become a place of growth?
5. What helps you take one more step when the journey feels overwhelming?

Prayer Prompt — Chapter 8: Heat of the Journey

- Lord, teach me to receive the refreshment You provide.
- Help me recognize when I need to stop and be renewed.
- Thank You for protecting me even when the desert remains.

CHAPTER 9

THE REFRESHMENT BOOTHS

Key Scripture: Psalm 23:3

The travelers first noticed them when exhaustion distorted the horizon. At a distance, the structures appeared small and unremarkable; simple shelters rising from the sand, thoughtfully placed along the road. Some passed by them at first, unsure whether they were meant for stopping or merely markers along the way. However, the need for shade became evident when the heat became unbearable. The beverage booths weren't extravagant. They served as provisions.

"He restores my soul; He leads me in paths of righteousness for His name's sake."
— **Psalm 23:3 NKJV**

The travelers found cool water, shade, and peacefulness within each booth, things the desert could never provide. The water restored bravery in addition to quenching their thirst. Weariness subsided. Strength returned. Even long- suppressed hope began to breathe again. Every booth was unique. Every booth was unique.

Some offered silence and stillness. Travelers were reminded of the reason behind their initial choice of route by the gentle words of truth echoed by others. On occasions, they encountered fellow travelers, who offered encouragement, testimonies, and prayers that felt like lifelines.

"Therefore encourage one another and build each other up."
— **1 Thessalonians 5:11 NIV**

The guide explained their purpose as they rested. "These places exist so you do not confuse exhaustion with failure", he said. "You were never meant to walk this road alone or without renewal."

"Come [away] with Me by yourselves to a quiet place and get some rest."
— **Mark 6:31 NIV**

Some travelers stayed longer than others. Fearing they might not reach another booth in time, some attempted to carry the water with them. The guide responded to their worry with a soft grin. He reminded them that the refreshment was intended to be consumed rather than kept. "Have faith that the provision will be there for you when you need it."

"Give us this day our daily bread."
— **Matthew 6:11 KJV**

As they stepped back onto the road, something changed. The desert remained. The sun continued to shine. However, the travelers' gait had changed; they were now lighter, steadier, and more assured. They were no longer characterized by the burden they had previously borne. Their strength came from what they had been given, not from themselves.

"Those who wait on the Lord shall renew their strength."
— **Isaiah 40:31 NKJV**

At that point, some came to see that the booths weren't a hindrance to the journey. They were crucial to it. They served as reminders that hard work was not enough to keep the road going. A reminder that every mile was laced with grace. It served as a reminder that the person who constructed the road also anticipated their vulnerability. And the travelers proceeded, one step closer to the Kingdom, one step closer to home, with revitalized hearts and strength.

Reflection Questions — Chapter 9: The Refreshment Booths

1. What do the refreshment booths represent in your walk with God?
2. Why is it sometimes difficult to stop and receive renewal?
3. How does community strengthen your spiritual journey?
4. What happens when we try to store grace instead of trusting daily provision?
5. Where do you currently need spiritual refreshment?

Prayer Prompt — Chapter 9: The Refreshment Booths

- Lord, help me recognize the refreshment You provide along my journey.
- Teach me to receive Your grace without guilt or fear.
- Show me how to be a source of encouragement to others on the road.

CHAPTER 10

COVERED IN THE DESERT

Key Scripture: Psalm 121:5–6

Those who continued along the road noticed something they could not explain. The desert had not changed; the sun rose and set with the same intensity. The sand still stretched endlessly in every direction. Yet the journey no longer crushed them the way it once had. They were still in the desert, but they were covered. The refreshments they had received did not fade when they left the booth.

At first, the covering was subtle. It did not announce itself. It did not remove hardship or erase discomfort. Instead, it revealed itself in what no longer happened. Fear no longer ruled their decisions. Despair no longer dictated their pace. Though exhaustion visited them, it no longer overtook them.

"The Lord is your keeper; the Lord is your shade at your right hand. The sun shall not strike you by day."
— **Psalm 121:5–6 NKJV**

The travelers began to understand that protection does not always look like escape. Sometimes it looks like endurance without destruction. Though the heat pressed down, it no longer burned them the way it once had. Though storms arose, they did not consume them. They walked differently now. Their steps carried confidence, not because the road was easier, but because they believed the One who had promised to protect them.

"When you pass through the waters, I will be with you... when you walk through the fire, you shall not be burned."
— **Isaiah 43:2 NKJV**

Others who watched from afar could not understand how they continued. They saw the same desert, the same heat, the same obstacles, but they could not see the covering. What sustained the travelers was invisible to the natural eye. Faith had placed a shield over them.

"Above all, take up the shield of faith."
— **Ephesians 6:16**

The desert, previously a place of fear, has evolved into a place of testimony. Every maneuver taken under protection confirmed that the road was operational. The King's promise had come true. The covering was held in place. It does not leave when you are doubtful. It exists because it was given, not earned. The travelers glanced at each other and realized something profound: the desert had not changed at all. They had. And, dressed in secured clothing that they had not designed, they marched steadily and confidently toward the point where the road would eventually give way to water.

Reflection Questions — Chapter 10: Covered in the Desert

1. What does it mean to be covered even while still in the desert?
2. How does understanding God's protection change how you face trials?
3. Why is it important to remember that the covering is given, not earned?
4. How have past wounds been transformed into testimonies in your life?
5. What would it look like to walk with confidence instead of fear?

Prayer Prompt — Chapter 10: Covered in the Desert

- Lord, thank You for covering me even when I cannot see it.
- Help me trust Your protection during trials and uncertainty.
- Teach me to walk boldly, knowing You go before me and stand behind me.

CHAPTER 11

THE POOL BEYOND WORDS

Key Scripture: 1 Corinthians 2:9

The path beneath them began to alter. The sand grew thinner. The air had chilled. What had felt never-ending before now bore a quiet expectation, as if the desert sensed its reign was coming to an end. The travelers slowed down, not because they were tired, but because they were in complete awe. Something sacred lay ahead. Then they saw it. The pool. It was more than just amazing; it was beyond extraordinary.

It stretched wider than imagined, its surface alive with light. The water mirrored not only the sky, but also the faces of people who stood before it: healed, entire, and unburdened. It was impervious to the scorching heat. Time appeared to bend in its presence.

"No eye has seen, no ear has heard, no mind has conceived what God has prepared for those who love Him."
— 1 Corinthians 2:9

As they got closer, memories surfaced of every mile walked, every tear shed, every doubt endured. The journey suddenly made sense. Not because the desert had been easy, but because the destination revealed its purpose. Some fell to their knees. Others wept openly.

Everyone realized the same truth: The pool was not merely a reward. It was restoration.

"He who was seated on the throne said, 'I am making everything new.'"
— **Revelation 21:5 NIV**

They entered the water cautiously at first, then completely. The moment it touched them, the weight of the desert dissolved. Scars faded, not erased but healed. Weariness gave way to strength deeper than anything they had known. This was the life they had been destined for.

"Whoever believes in Me,... rivers of living water will flow from within them."
— **John 7:38 NIV**

Laughter returned, uninhibited and widespread. The child's dream had been fulfilled at last. Brothers and sisters filled the pool, sharing joy that did not diminish after being given away. Then they noticed him. The One who built the road standing at the edge of the pool. No longer marked by exhaustion or sacrifice, He stood clothed in glory. The desert did not defeat Him. Death had not held Him. The King smiled, not as a distant ruler, but as a victorious Savior who welcomed His people home.

"Worthy is the Lamb who was slain."
— **Revelation 5:12 NIV**

They bowed, not out of fear, but gratitude. For in that moment, they understood, the road was never just about reaching the pool. It was about being reunited with the King.

Reflection Questions — Chapter 11: The Pool Beyond Words

1. What emotions arise when you imagine arriving at the pool?
2. How does the image of restoration change your understanding of eternity?
3. Why is healing described as restoration rather than replacement?
4. How does joy multiply when it is shared?
5. In what ways does the hope of what's ahead strengthen you today?

Prayer Prompt — Chapter 11: The Pool Beyond Words

- Lord, thank You for the promise of restoration and eternal life.
- Help me live today with my eyes fixed on what is to come.
- Fill me with joy that sustains me until the journey is complete.

THE KING WHO BUILT THE WAY

Key Scripture: Hebrews 12:2

The pool shimmered with life, but the travelers' eyes remained laser-focused on the One standing beside it. They had followed the road to its end, but now they understood the road had always led to Him. The King stood there, not distant, not unapproachable, but present. The same One who had sacrificed time, strength, and Himself to pave the way now welcomed them as family. The desert no longer separated them. The road had accomplished its intended purpose. His eyes had shown no trace of regret. Only joy.

"For the joy set before Him, He endured the cross."
— **Hebrews 12:2 NIV**

"Therefore, God exalted Him to the highest place and gave Him the name that is above every name."
— **Philippians 2:9 NIV**

The King glanced at those who had arrived and acknowledged every stage of their journey. He had witnessed their doubt, the weariness, and moments when they were on the verge of giving up. None of it surprised Him. None of it disqualified them. What mattered was that they had arrived.

They were aware that the sacrifice didn't end after the road was finished. The true cost was leaving the pool to build the road in the first place. The King had ventured into the desert so others could return to the Kingdom. The silence was saturated with compassion. Worship rose naturally, like breath after being held too long. This was the Kingdom they had forgotten. Not merely a place, but a presence. Not only water, but life itself.

"For the Son of Man came to seek and to save the lost."
— **Luke 19:10 NIV**

The King stepped toward them, inviting them to fully embrace the life the road had promised. The pool mirrored both their faces and His faithfulness. They were no longer strangers or travelers. They were home.

"In My Father's house are many rooms."
— **John 14:2**

"Behold, the dwelling place of God is with man."
— **Revelation 21:3 ESV**

The King stepped into the pool with them. Joy overflowed. Fellowship restored the distance that had been stolen. The desert, once huge and cruel, became a testimony of salvation. As they stood together, refreshed and whole, they discovered something profound: Redemption. The King who paved the way has been waiting all along.

Reflection Questions — Chapter 12: The King Who Built the Way

1. What does it mean to you that the King is the same One who built the road?
2. How does seeing Jesus as both Sacrifice and King deepen your understanding of salvation?
3. Why is gratitude, rather than fear or obligation, the natural response to the King in this chapter?
4. In what ways does this chapter redefine what "home" means spiritually?
5. How does knowing the road was built out of love change how you view your own journey?

Prayer Prompt — Chapter 12: The King Who Built The Way

- King Jesus, thank You for making a way back to the Father.
- Help me live as someone who has been restored, not rescued reluctantly.
- Teach me to worship You with gratitude, obedience, and love.

CLOSING PRAYER

Gracious Father,

Thank You for making a way back to You when none existed. Thank You for the road built through the desert, for the sacrifice that finished the work, and for the grace that carries us every step of the journey.

For every reader who has walked this road through these pages, meet them where they are. Refresh the weary. Strengthen the discouraged. Heal the wounded. Remind us that we are not saved by how far we can walk, but by trusting the One who built the way.

Teach us to live as people of the Kingdom even while we remain in the desert, covered, guided, and sustained by Your love. May we never forget that the road was built not only to bring us home, but also to invite others to follow.

We bow in gratitude, we stand in hope, and we walk forward in faith. In the name of Jesus, the Way, the Truth, and the Life.

Amen.

BENEDICTION

May you walk the road with courage, knowing it has already been finished. May you find refreshment when the heat presses in, and protection when the desert rises against you. May the presence of the King go before you, the guidance of the Spirit walk beside you, and the peace of God cover you until the journey is complete. And may you live each day as one who has found the way back to God's Kingdom.

Amen.